MACHINES ★ AT WORK

TRAINS

BY HAL ROGERS

THE CHILD'S WORLD® • MANKATO, MINNESOTA

The Child's World

Published in the United States of America by The Child's World®
1980 Lookout Drive • Mankato, MN 56003-1705
800-599-READ • www.childsworld.com

PHOTO CREDITS
© David M. Budd Photography: 7 (main)
© David R. Frazier Photolibrary, Inc./Alamy: 19 (main)
© iStockphoto.com/Alex Harris: 3
© iStockphoto.com/Corstiaan van Elzelingen: cover, 2
© iStockphoto.com/Furchin: 15
© iStockphoto.com/Heiko Bennewitz: 20
© iStockphoto.com/Kenneth Sponsler: 8
© iStockphoto.com/Klaus Nilkens: 7 (inset)
© iStockphoto.com/Majoros Laszlo: 16
© iStockphoto.com/Steve Krull: 4
© Mark Ralston/Reuters/Corbis: 19 (inset)
© Philip Gould/Corbis: 11
© Rob Wilkinson/Alamy: 12

ACKNOWLEDGMENTS
The Child's World®: Mary Berendes, Publishing Director;
Katherine Stevenson, Editor

The Design Lab: Design and Page Production

LIBRARY OF CONGRESS CATALOGING-IN-PUBLICATION DATA
Rogers, Hal, 1966–
    Trains / by Hal Rogers.
        p. cm. — (Machines at work)
    Includes bibliographical references and index.
    ISBN 978-1-59296-960-9 (library bound : alk. paper)
    1. Railroads—Juvenile literature. [1. Railroads—Trains.] I. Title. II. Series.
    TF148.R65 2007
    625.1—dc22   2007013407

⭐ Contents

This train is traveling in Colorado. ★

What are trains?

Trains are **vehicles** that move along a track. Train cars travel along metal rails. The cars are hooked together in a line.

How are trains used?

Passenger trains take people from place to place. These trains have seats and windows. Some passenger trains travel long distances. They often have a dining car where people can eat. They sometimes have sleeping cars, too.

The main photo shows people boarding a passenger train. The small photo shows the inside.

Here you can see two freight trains. The long one is carrying boxes of goods. The shorter one is carrying coal.

Other trains carry goods, or **freight**. Freight trains carry heavy loads for long distances. Different types of freight cars carry different kinds of goods.

Some freight cars keep food cool. Some carry big metal boxes that hold lots of goods. Others have bins for carrying coal or other rock. Some have air holes for carrying animals.

This locomotive is waiting for its next load.

electric wires

This train gets its power from electricity.
You can see the wires overhead.

Who drives a train?

A train's driver is called an **engineer**. The engineer sits in the **cab**. The cab has **controls** for running the train.

How do trains move?

Some train cars have their own **engine**. The engine provides power so the car can move. Other train cars are pulled or pushed by a **locomotive**. Locomotives have big, powerful engines. They can pull lots of weight.

This engineer is driving a passenger train in England. You can see all the controls he needs to use.

★ Here you can see many kinds of freight cars!
Can you guess what some of them are carrying?

Many train engines get their power from burning **diesel fuel**. Others get their power from **electricity**. Sometimes the electricity comes through overhead wires. Sometimes it comes through a rail on the track.

Most trains have metal wheels on the bottom. The wheels roll along metal rails. Some trains do not have wheels. Instead, magnets hold them above the rails.

⭐ The main photo shows a train's wheel moving along the rail. The smaller photo shows a train in China. It is held up by magnets.

"Bullet trains" like this one go very fast. In fact, they can go 277 miles (446 km) an hour! Bullet trains are passenger trains.

Are trains important?

Trains are used all over the world. They carry heavy goods over long distances. They take people from place to place quickly. Trains are very important!

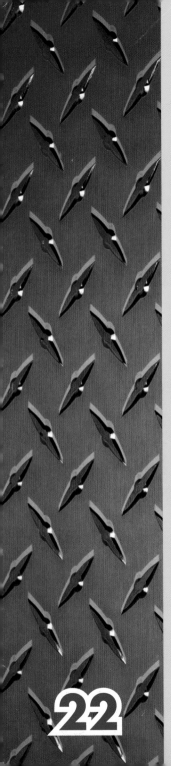

 # Glossary

cab (KAB) A machine's cab is the area where the driver sits.

controls (kun-TROLZ) Controls are parts that people use to run a machine.

diesel fuel (DEE-sul FYOOL) Diesel fuel is a heavy oil that is burned to make power.

electricity (ee-lek-TRIH-sih-tee) Electricity is a kind of power or energy.

engine (EN-jun) An engine is a machine that makes something move.

engineer (en-juh-NEER) On trains, an engineer is a person who runs the engine.

freight (FRAYT) Freight is a name for goods carried on a ship, plane, train, or truck.

locomotive (loh-kuh-MO-tiv) A locomotive is a train car that can push or pull other cars.

passenger (PASS-un-jur) A passenger is a person who rides in something.

vehicles (VEE-uh-kullz) Vehicles are things for carrying people or goods.

 # Books

Balkwill, Richard. *The Best Book of Trains.* New York: Kingfisher, 1999.

Harding, Mary, and Richard Courtney (illustrator). *All Aboard Trains.* New York: Platt & Munk, 1989.

National Railway Museum. *Big Book of Trains.* New York: DK Publishing, 1998.

Simon, Seymour. *Seymour Simon's Book of Trains.* New York: HarperCollins Publishers, 2004.

 # Web Sites

Visit our Web page for lots of links about trains:
http://www.childsworld.com/links
Note to parents, teachers, and librarians: We routinely check our Web links to make sure they're safe, active sites—so encourage your readers to check them out!

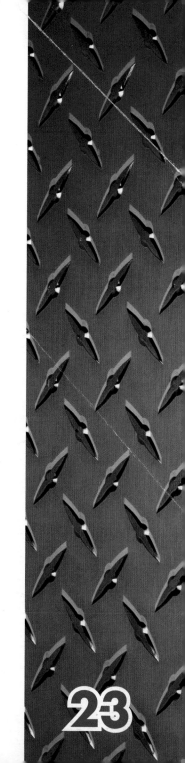

 # Index

 # About the Author

Hal Rogers has written over a dozen books on machines and trucks. A longtime resident of Colorado, Hal currently lives in Denver, along with his family, a fuzzy cat named Simon, and a lovable dog named Sebastian.